NATURE CLOSE-UP

Carnivorous Plants

TEXT BY ELAINE PASCOE

PHOTOGRAPHS BY DWIGHT KUHN

BLACKBIRCH PRESS
An imprint of Thomson Gale, a part of The Thomson Corporation

THOMSON

GALE

Detroit • New York • San Francisco • San Diego • New Haven, Conn. • Waterville, Maine • London • Munich

LIBRARY OF CONGRESS CATALOGING-IN-PUBLICATION DATA

Pascoe, Elaine.
 Carnivorous Plants / by Elaine Pascoe ; photographs by Dwight Kuhn.
     p. cm. — (Nature close-up)
 Includes index.
 ISBN 1-4103-0309-8 (alk. paper)
 1. Plants-carnivorous —Juvenile literature. I. Kuhn, Dwight. II. Title III. Series: Pascoe, Elaine. Nature close-up.

Printed in China
10 9 8 7 6 5 4 3 2 1

Contents

❋ ❋ ❋

1
• • •
Plants Bite Back!

A plant that eats animals—that sounds like something from a scary science-fiction story. Nature usually works the other way around: Animals eat plants. But a few plants turn this natural order on its head. They are **carnivorous** (meat eating) plants.

Carnivorous plants make up only a small segment of our planet's plant life. Some of these plants are very rare. Others are more common. You might even find carnivorous plants growing near your home—if you live near a bog or a swamp. Most of these

These plants seem harmless, but they are deadly traps for insects.

fascinating and unusual plants grow in wetlands.

Hungry Plants

There's nothing scary about carnivorous plants. These plants don't eat "meat" as we think of it. They mostly trap and digest small insects, although a few types grow large enough to manage a small frog or lizard. The plants consume animal life for a simple reason: to get **nutrients** that they desperately need.

Most plants make their own food through a process called **photosynthesis**. Their leaves contain **chlorophyll** and other pigments,

Carnivorous plants, such as these pitcher plants, trap animals to get nutrients they need.

which capture the energy in sunlight. The plant uses this energy to turn water and carbon dioxide, which it draws from the air, into a type of sugar. The sugar is the plant's food, fueling its growth. But to thrive, plants must also have certain other nutrients, such as nitrogen. Most plants get these nutrients from the soil, through their roots.

Carnivorous plants have chlorophyll and can carry out photosynthesis. But in the places where these plants generally grow, the soil is often very low in nutrients. Nitrogen and other nutrients are found in animal tissues, however. By consuming insects and whatever else they can catch, the plants make up for the poor soil of their habitat.

It's not easy to catch insects, however. Just try to swat a fly!

A flower fly can't escape from a sticky sundew.

For a plant, which is rooted in one place, the task is even harder. The plant can't chase its prey, so it lures insects to its leaves. The leaves are traps. Once an insect lands on one of these leaf traps, its fate is sealed.

There are several main groups of carnivorous plants, and each has its own way of attracting and trapping prey.

Goodbye, fly: A venus flytrap prepares to close its trap.

Pitcher Plants

A pitcher plant's insect trap is a special leaf shaped like a long tube, often with a flap arching over the opening at the top. In many plants the rim of the tube is colorful, so it resembles a flower. It is baited with a

Special tube-shaped leaves form the traps of a pitcher plant.

9

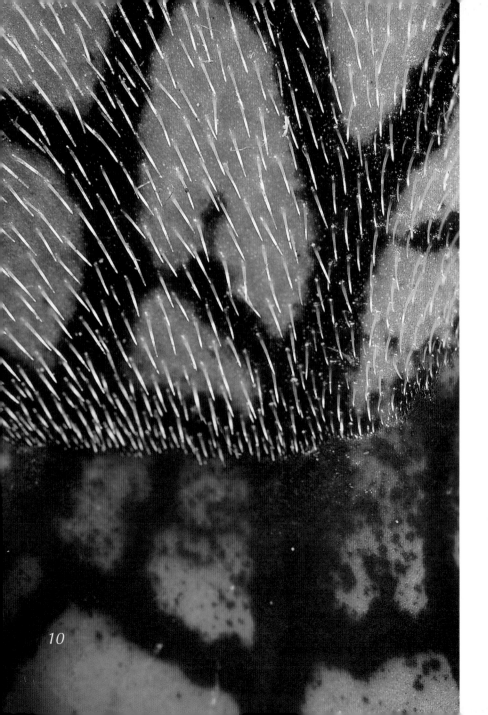

slick, sweet **secretion** that insects mistake for flower nectar.

Hoping for a meal of nectar, an insect is drawn to the pitcher. It flies or crawls to the rim, where the secretion draws it into the trap. The inner walls of the tube are slippery and covered with stiff hairs, all pointing down. They keep the insect

The pitcher's slippery inner walls are covered with stiff hairs that keep insects from climbing out.

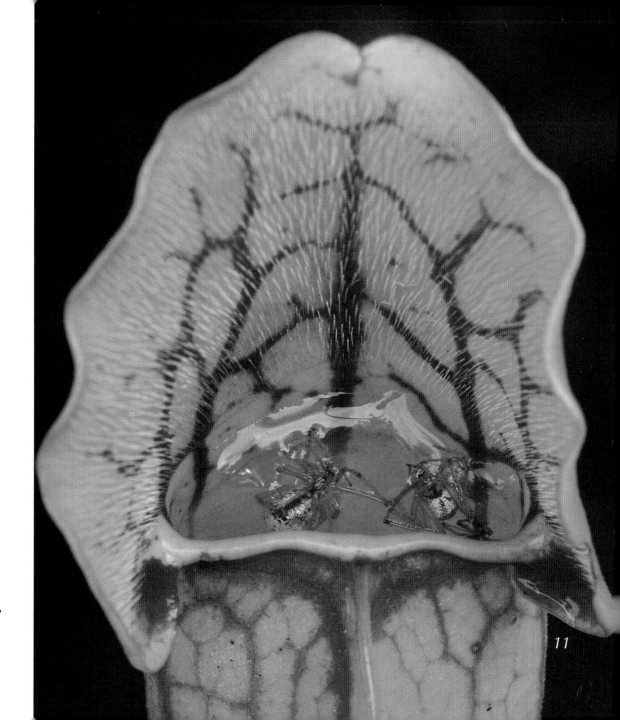

from crawling up and out. The insect slides deeper and deeper into the tube, until it finally falls to the bottom.

The bottom of the tube holds a little pool of water mixed with digestive juices that the plant produces. The digestive juices break down the insect's body, and the plant absorbs the nutrients that it needs. Eventually only the shell of the insect is left, floating in the

Two spiders are trapped in the water and digestive juices inside a pitcher plant.

11

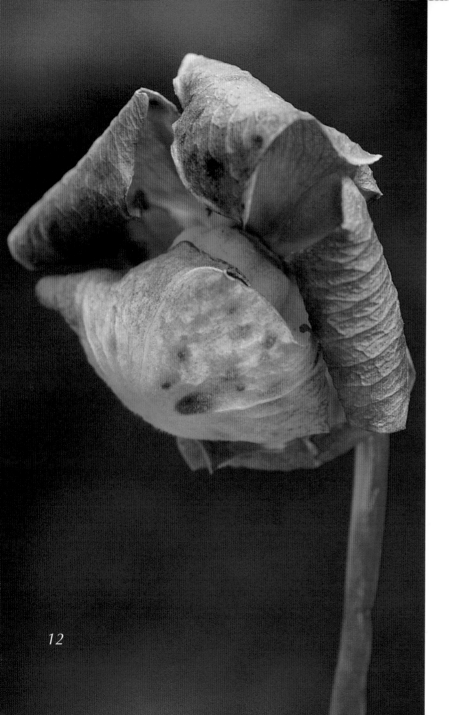

pool. Over time the base of the pitcher becomes cluttered with the remains of insects and spiders that fall victim to its trap.

Several types of pitcher plants grow wild in the wetlands of North America. New pitchers grow from the base of these plants each year, sometimes reaching 2 to 3 feet (about 60 to 90 cm) tall. Depending on the variety, the plants produce purple or yellow flowers in the spring. The flowers are the first step in the plants' reproductive cycle. After **pollination**, the flower fades and seeds begin to form. What was the base of the flower develops into a seedpod. When the seeds are ready, the pod breaks open, and the seeds scatter. Those that land in good, boggy spots will grow into new pitcher plants.

The pitcher plant's unusual flowers appear in spring.

Cobra Plants

One look tells you how the cobra plant got its name. This plant's most obvious feature is a tall, curled leaf that looks like the head of a hooded cobra, raised and ready to strike. Part of the leaf even extends like a snake's forked tongue.

The cobra plant is a variation of the pitcher plant, and the curled leaf is the plant's insect trap. The cobra's tongue drips with sweet nectar that lures insects. Insects land on the tongue and crawl up into the hood, which holds more nectar. They don't realize that they are entering a trap. The top of the hood is **translucent** and allows light to enter, so they think it's open. But once inside, the insects can't get out. They slip and fall down to the pool of water at the bottom of the tube. Those that try to climb out are forced back by downward-pointing hairs that line the walls.

Unlike most other carnivorous plants, cobra plants don't produce digestive juices. But the water inside their tubes is full of bacteria. The bacteria break down the plant's insect prey, and plant and bacteria alike get the nutrients they need.

These unusual plants grow wild only in western Oregon and northern California. They are also known as cobra lilies and California pitcher plants. Cobra plants like damp soil, and they can often be found along the edges of streams. Their purplish or yellow flowers rise above the leaf traps on tall stems.

The cobra plant's trap looks like the head of a hooded cobra, complete with a forked tongue.

13

14

Sundews

A sundew's leaves are covered with reddish hairs. At the tip of each hair is a glob of sticky nectar. The globs of nectar glisten in the sun like dewdrops—which is how the sundew got its name—and attract hungry insects. But when an insect lands on a sundew leaf, its feet become stuck in the gluelike secretion. The harder the insect struggles, the more firmly it is trapped.

Slowly, the hairs on the edge of the leaf curl around over the insect, so that it can't escape. The leaf begins to secrete digestive juices, and the sundew has a meal. When the insect is completely digested, the leaf uncurls and begins to make more glistening bait.

Sundews make up a big group of carnivorous plants. There are about 160 different

A sundew leaf curls around a trapped moth and begins to digest it.

15

kinds of these plants, and they are found in every part of the world except the Arctic and Antarctica. Australia and southern Africa have the most sundews.

There is a lot of variety in the sundew family. Leaves may be round or shaped like teaspoons or tentacles. The king sundew of southern Africa has straplike leaves that can grow up to 2 feet (about 60 cm) long. In cold climates most sundews are small plants. The most widespread sundew in North America is the round-leafed sundew. Its leaves are about the size and shape of dimes, and it bears white flowers on stems about 10 inches (25 cm) tall.

The hairs on a sundew leaf are tipped with globs of nectar. Sundew leaves come in many shapes and sizes, but they are all deadly traps.

The Venus Flytrap

The venus flytrap is a member of the sundew family. These plants are very rare in the wild—they grow only in a few boggy places along the Carolina coast. They are especially fascinating because they catch insects in fast-moving traps.

The flytrap is a small plant, with white flowers that grow on a stalk about a foot (30 cm) tall. The leaves branch out from the base of the plant, and they may be 6 inches (15 cm) long. Each leaf ends in a pair of lobes that look something like the two halves of a clamshell. Each lobe is fringed with long, sharp spines.

To a hungry insect, the leaves of a venus flytrap look like flowers.

17

The lobes are the plant's traps. They sit open, facing upward, displaying an inner surface coated with a sticky secretion insects can't resist. An insect lands on the leaf and begins moving around in search of a meal. Then, suddenly, the lobes snap together. Their spines lock the insect inside.

A very small insect may still be able to wiggle out between the spines, but larger insects are doomed. Within minutes the lobes press tightly together and begin to secrete digestive juices. The insect is crushed, and its body is broken down. The flytrap may take anywhere from one to ten days to digest its meal. Then it opens the lobes, resetting its trap for a new victim. Each leaf trap can catch only about four insects before it dies.

What triggers the trap? As an insect moves around on the lobe, it brushes against sensitive hairs. There are six of these hairs on the inner surface of each lobe. If the insect touches one hair, nothing happens. This way, the trap won't shut every time a speck of dust lands on the lobe. But if two hairs are touched, or if one is touched twice in quick succession, the trap snaps shut. Scientists think the hairs trigger a chemical reaction inside the leaf, and this reaction causes the lobes to fold together.

A flytrap leaf closes around a damselfly.

Inset: The inner surface of the leaf has tiny trigger hairs. If an insect brushes two hairs, the trap shuts.

19

TROPICAL PITCHERS

Pitcher plants grow in many other parts of the world. In the tropical rain forests of Borneo and other Asian and Pacific lands, exotic pitcher plants called *Nepenthes* grow as vines that climb trees or creep along the ground. Their pitchers develop at the tips of their flat leaves.

These tropical pitchers often have colorful patterns. Like North American pitchers, they produce nectar that attracts prey. The insides of the pitchers are slick and covered with downward-pointing hairs that make it difficult for prey to escape. The traps of some types of tropical pitchers are big enough to trap frogs or even small rodents!

This colorful tropical pitcher plant grows in the rain forests of Borneo, in Southeast Asia.

Butterworts are small plants that grow in swampy places in most northern countries. The common butterwort of North America has purple flowers on tall stems. It's sometimes called the bog violet.

The common butterwort's yellow-green leaves grow from the base of the plant, in the form of a rosette. They're covered with fine hairs, and their edges curl up. And like the leaves of sundews, they're covered with sticky secretions. The leaves feel greasy, or buttery, to the touch, and that's how the butterworts got their name.

The butterwort draws insects with a musty odor that has been described as smelling like mushrooms or cheese. Insects land on the sticky leaves and find themselves trapped. Large insects can usually break free from the butterwort's glue, but small insects such as gnats and mayflies aren't strong enough to get away. The leaf slowly curls around its victim and begins to secrete digestive juices. In a few days, when the plant has finished its meal, the leaf uncurls. The leaves of a butterwort are often littered with the shells of insects that the plant has digested.

Butterworts don't react when grains of sand or other nonfood items land on their leaves. But they do curl up and digest grains of pollen and bits of seeds. Somehow, the plant is able to tell what's food and what's not.

The common butterwort's purple flower rises above its sticky leaves, which are insect traps.

21

Bladderworts

Most bladderworts are water plants that grow in lakes, ponds, and bogs. These plants have no true roots. They float in the water, at or below the surface, looking like tangles of greenish thread. The tangles are networks of thin branching stems and small threadlike leaves.

Attached to the leaves are tiny hollow bladders that look like little balloons. Most of the bladders are no more than an eighth of an inch (3mm) across. They help the plant stay afloat, but their main job is to trap prey. Sensitive hairs rim the mouth of each bladder. It has a trap door that opens only one way—in.

The bladderwort's traps look like tiny balloons.

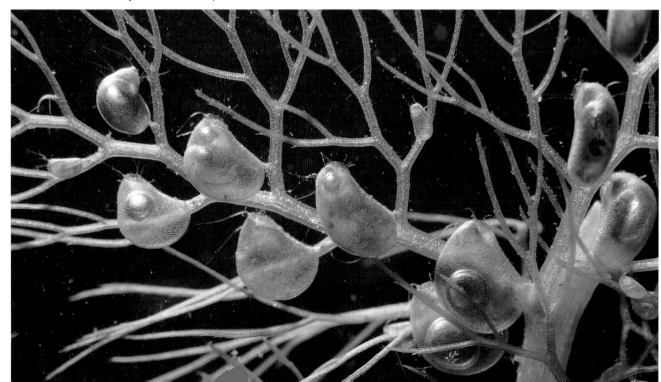

The bladderwort's traps spring open to suck in tiny animals like this mosquito larva.

The bladderwort preys on tiny underwater animals such as mosquito **larvae** and water fleas. These creatures swim among the plant's stems and leaves, looking for food or shelter. When one brushes against the sensitive hairs at the mouth of a bladder, the walls of the bladder suddenly expand. This creates suction that opens the door and sucks the prey inside. Then the door slams shut, and the plant digests its meal.

There are about 200 different kinds of bladderworts, including a few that grow on land. They are flowering plants, and the flowers of those that live in water are carried on stems that rise above the surface. The common bladderwort of North America and Europe has attractive yellow flowers, and it's sometimes grown in garden ponds for that reason. But the real action is underwater.

Carnivorous Plants and People

Many types of carnivorous plants are rare, and some are in danger of dying out. In many places the swamps where the plants live have been drained to build homes or roads or to create farmland, destroying their habitat. These plants are also very sensitive to pollution.

Collection is another problem. Pitcher plants, venus flytraps, and other carnivorous plants are such curiosities that people often want to dig them up and take them home. But when people collect rare plants this way, too few may remain in the wild for the species to survive.

The rarest carnivorous plants are protected by law, and it's illegal to dig them up. Many areas now have laws protecting wetlands, too. The laws will help ensure that these strange and fascinating plants don't disappear.

Many people are fascinated by rare carnivorous plants, such as this tropical pitcher.

CAN'T CATCH ME!

Some animals can escape the traps of carnivorous plants. Certain types of ants and true bugs can move around freely on sticky sundew leaves, for instance. They may steal the prey from the plant's trap, but the plant doesn't lose. The visiting insects leave droppings that are rich in minerals, and the plant absorbs the minerals through its leaves.

Insect eaters such as frogs sometimes hang out near carnivorous plants, hoping to catch insects that are drawn to the plants. Some spiders spin webs across the mouths of pitchers, to catch insects that are drawn to the plant. But the spider must be careful not to fall in!

Some insects can live inside the pitcher traps. A type of flesh fly lays its eggs right in the pitcher trap. When the fly larvae hatch, they produce a substance that protects them from the plant's digestive juices. Then they feed on insects and spiders that have fallen into the trap. When they are ready to pupate and become adults, they bore holes through the side of the pitcher to get out.

A tree frog waits at a pitcher plant's mouth, hoping to catch an insect.

The larvae of certain mosquitoes live in some pitcher plants, too. As adults, the mosquitoes are able to fly in and out of the trap like little helicopters, never getting caught.

2

Growing Carnivorous Plants

Carnivorous plants are great subjects for close-up study. They're not easy to find in nature, and so it's not always possible to observe them in the wild. But you can learn about these plants by growing specimens that you buy.

Plants such as venus flytraps are available in stores and through mail-order sources like those listed on page 45. Don't collect wild plants, and don't buy from sources that collect wild plants. Buy only plants that have been grown in greenhouses. Wild plants should be left in the wild, so they can form seeds and reproduce.

Some carnivorous plants can be tricky to grow. But your plants will thrive if you give them the conditions that they need. Remember that these plants are used to lots of moisture and soil that is low in nutrients. This section will tell you how to care for a venus flytrap, one of the most popular plants.

Feeding flies to a venus flytrap is part of the fun of keeping this plant.

27

Setting the flytrap's pot in a tray of water gives the plant the moisture it needs.

Planting a Venus Flytrap

If you order a venus flytrap through the mail, it may arrive in a **dormant** (resting) state. You will need to pot it. Fill a small flowerpot with sphagnum moss, which you can get at any garden center. The moss is better than regular soil or potting soil mixtures, which will be too rich in nutrients for the plant.

Plant the venus flytrap in the moss. The roots and lower part of the bulb should be covered by moss, but don't bury the plant too deeply.

Evenly moisten the moss with distilled water, which you can find at grocery and drug stores, or rainwater. Don't use tap water. Flytraps are very sensitive to chemicals and minerals that may be in tap water.

Place the flowerpot into a larger container. Add distilled water to this container until it covers the base of the flowerpot, to a height of about an inch (2.5 cm).

Place the container in a warm place with bright but not direct sunlight. As the water level in the large container goes down, add more distilled water, so the moss won't dry out.

Your plant may need may need some time to adjust to its new home. Leaves may turn brown, and the plant may appear to be dying. Give the plant a few weeks to begin producing new growth.

Making a Terrarium

Terrariums are great for growing venus flytraps and some other carnivorous plants indoors because they hold moisture, which these plants love. To make a terrarium, you'll need a clear container such as a small fish tank or a large wide-mouthed glass jar. The shape of the container does not matter.

Put a layer of loose gravel in the bottom, for drainage. Next, make a mixture of one part clean store sand and two parts dried peat moss. Be sure that the peat moss has no added fertilizer. Put a layer of this mixture several inches deep over the gravel. Moisten the mixture with distilled water, using a sprayer to get it evenly damp. Then top the peat-moss mixture with a layer of sphagnum moss.

Above: Gravel is the bottom layer in a terrarium.

Left: Mix clean sand and peat moss for the second layer.

29

Plant your venus flytraps so that the roots are in the peat-moss mixture and covered with a thin layer of sphagnum moss. Add distilled water or rainwater as the top layer starts to dry out. To make it easy to water the plants without disturbing the mixture around their roots, place loose stones in one corner. Pour water over the loose stones, and it will filter into the peat moss mixture.

If your terrarium has a large opening at the top, you can partly cover it with a clear plastic cover. The cover will keep moisture around the leaves. Don't cover the container completely, though—the plants need some fresh air to stay healthy. Containers with small openings don't need any covering.

Put your terrarium in a warm place with bright light, but not in direct sunlight. Strong sunlight may overheat the terrarium and "cook" your plants.

Stones in a corner of the terrarium give you a place to add water without disturbing the plant roots.

Caring for Your Plants

Venus flytraps don't need a lot of care. Keep their containers moist with distilled water or rainwater. Never use fertilizer, which could harm these plants.

You can feed a fly or another medium-sized insect to your plants about once a month. Use tweezers to put the fly directly on a trap. If your plant is in a terrarium, add the fly to the container and cover the top until the insect is caught.

One fly a month is all that most venus flytrap plants need.

A monthly fly gives the plant extra nourishment. However, the plant can survive without flies—and it may catch insects on its own. Feeding more flies won't help the plant grow and may even weaken it. Don't feed your plant bits of hamburger or other fatty foods. The plant can't digest these foods, and the leaves will rot.

It's fun to play with the traps and trick them into closing by tapping the trigger hairs with a toothpick. But don't overdo it. Remember that each trap can close only four times or so before it dies.

After adding a fly, cover your container with mesh so that the insect can't escape.

In the wild, venus flytraps are dormant in winter. They stop growing, and old leaves turn brown and die. During this time the plant stores energy for the coming year. Give your plants a similar rest. When its leaves begin to die in the fall, put the plants in a place that's cool but not below freezing. The plants will need less light and less water during this time, but don't let the containers dry out completely. The plants should rest for about ninety days. In spring, bring them back to a warm, brightly lighted place and give them more water. They will soon put out new growth.

Venus flytraps usually grow new leaves in the spring, after a winter rest.

3

Investigating Carnivorous Plants

Once your venus flytraps have settled into their new home, you can begin to learn more about these plants and their strange eating habits. In this chapter you'll find some activities and experiments that will help you answer some questions. Some of the experiments call for two plants in separate containers, but other activities can be done with just one plant.

Do Venus Flytraps Digest Live Prey or Killed Prey More Easily?

Will a flytrap consume killed insects that you give it, or must its prey be live? Based on what you know about the way the plant's traps work, decide what you think. Then do this experiment to see if you are right.

What to Do:

1. Kill one fly by swatting it. Catch the live fly in a jar, and cover the top of the jar. Put the jar with the live fly in the refrigerator for a little while. The cold temperature will slow the insect down.

What You Need:
- Dead fly
- Live fly
- Two venus flytraps, both about the same size.
- Small jar with a cover
- Tweezers

2. Using tweezers, drop the dead fly onto a trap on one venus flytrap.
3. Also with tweezers, place the live fly onto a trap on the other plant.
4. Watch to see what the plants do.

Results: Note which traps close, how far they close, and how long they stay closed.

Conclusion: Did your results show a difference between the dead and live prey? If so, what do you think was the reason?

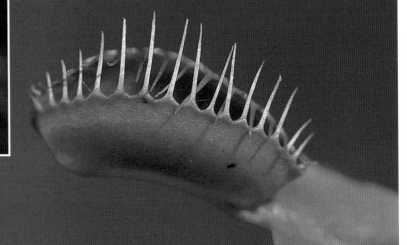

Do Venus Flytraps Grow Better with or Without Insect Meals?

Venus flytraps get nutrients from the insects they catch, but how important are the insects to the plants? Make your best guess, and then do this activity to find out.

What to Do:

1. Set your plants side by side so they'll both receive the same amount of light.
2. Feed a fly to one plant as described in chapter 2. Give the other plant no flies.
3. Cover the plants so that they don't catch insects on their own. (The plants are sometimes sold with plastic covers. You can also use a plastic cup as a cover.)
4. Continue this experiment for several months. Each month, feed a fly to one plant (always the same one), and give the other plant none. Remember to keep the plants well watered, as described in chapter 2.

Results: Compare the plants each month, and take notes about their condition. Note new growth, dying leaves, and overall color and appearance.

Conclusion: Does one plant grow better than the other? What do your results tell you about the plants' need for insects?

What You Need:
- Two venus flytraps, both about the same size.
- Covers for the plant containers
- Flies

What You Need:

- Two venus flytrap plants, in separate containers, with the same number of open traps
- Covers for the plant containers
- Flies
- Tweezers

Do Venus Flytraps Catch Flies Better in the Day or At Night?

A venus flytrap's traps are set twenty-four hours a day. Will the plant have more success trapping insects during the day or at night? Decide what you think, and then test your answer with this activity.

What to Do:

1. During daylight hours, put two flies into one plant container. Don't place the flies on traps. Just lift one side of the cover, release the flies, and quickly replace the cover so they can't get out.
2. At night, put two flies in the other container
3. Check the plants every few hours to see if they have caught flies.

Results: Note when each plant traps flies. Which plant has the most success?

Conclusion: What do your results tell you about the importance of daylight for trapping insects?

38

Will Traps Reopen Faster After Closing on Large Flies or Small Flies?

The traps on a venus flytrap close to catch prey and reopen after the plant has digested its meal. Does the size of the prey make a difference in how long a trap stays closed? Make your best guess, and then do this activity to see if you are right.

What to Do:

1. Using tweezers, place a small fly in one trap and a large fly in another.
2. Check to see when the traps reopen. This may take anywhere from several days to more than a week.

Results: Note whether one trap opens first, and which size fly it held.

Conclusion: What do your results tell you about the flytrap's digestion? Repeat the experiment using different kinds of prey that are all about the same size. For example, use a fly and a millipede or an earwig, or a caterpillar and a slug. Which is digested faster?

More Activities with Carnivorous Plants

1. Tickle a flytrap with a brush to see what makes the trap close. Touch the stem, spines, outside, and inside of a trap. What do you need to do to trigger the trap? When a plant closes without prey, how long does it take to reopen?
2. How long does it take for your plant to catch a fly? An ant? Put an insect in the plant's container, replace the cover, and time it.
3. Do carnivorous plants grow wild near your home? Check with the staff at nearby conservation societies, natural history museums, and wildlife refuges. See if you can arrange to see these plants in their habitats. Botanical gardens may have examples of exotic carnivorous plants, too.
4. Try your hand at growing other carnivorous plants. Pitcher plants, sundews, and other types of insect-trapping plants available in some stores and through mail-order sources like those listed on page 45. Never collect wild plants, though, and remember to buy only plants that have been grown in greenhouses.

Result and Conclusions

Here are some possible results and conclusions for the activities on pages 34 to 40. Because many conditions affect the way carnivorous plants grow, you may not get the same results. If your outcomes differ, try to think of reasons why. What do you think led to your results? Repeat the activity, and see if the outcome is the same.

Do venus flytraps digest live prey or killed prey more easily?
To digest an insect, a venus flytrap has to close its trap completely around its victim. Dead insects will cause the trap to close part way if they touch the trap's trigger hairs when placed in the trap. Live insects will trip the hairs repeatedly as they struggle to escape, causing the trap to close completely. Only then does digestion begin.

Do venus flytraps grow better with or without insect meals?

The plant that gets flies should grow better because it is getting extra nourishment. But you may not see a big difference right away. These plants normally grow in poor soils and can live for quite a while without insects.

Do venus flytraps catch flies better in the day or at night?

There may or may not be any difference. The traps are triggered by touch, not light, so they should close during the day or at night. If the flies are more active in one container and move around more, they may be trapped more quickly.

Will traps reopen faster after closing on large flies or small flies?

The small flies will probably be digested faster. With a smaller body, there is less material to digest.

Some Words About Carnivorous Plants

carnivorous Meat eating.

chlorophyll A green pigment that allows plants to use energy from sunlight to make food.

dormant Resting.

larvae Immature forms of insects.

nutrients Anything that a living thing needs to live and grow.

photosynthesis A process by which a plant makes its own food.

pollination Transfer of plant pollen (male cells) to the ovule, the part of the flower that holds eggs (female cells).

pupate Change from larval to adult form.

secretion A substance produced by glands in a plant or animal.

translucent Allowing light to pass through.

Sources for Carnivorous Plants

These companies sell carnivorous plants and supplies through the mail.

Carolina Biological Supply Company
2700 York Rd.
Burlington, NC 27215
(800) 334-5551
www.carosci.com

Connecticut Valley Biological Supply
82 Valley Rd., PO Box 326
Southampton, MA 01073
(800) 628-7748
www.ctvalleybio.com

Dangerous Plants
PO Box 3146
Falls Church, VA 22043
www.dangerousplants.com

Plants for Kids
Vista, California 92084
(760) 630-4170
www.plantsforkids.com

For More Information

Books

Densey Clyne, *Plants of Prey.* Milwaukee, WI: Gareth Stevens, 2002.

Kim T. Griswell, *Carnivorous Plants.* San Diego, CA: KidHaven Press, 2002.

L. Patricia Kite, *Insect-Eating Plants.* Minneapolis, MN: Millbrook Press, 1995.

D.M. Souza, *Meat-Eating Plants.* Danbury, CT: Franklin Watts, 2002.

Web sites

Dangerous Plants
(www.dangerousplants.com)
Click on "Growing Guide" for details
on caring for different carnivorous plants.

International Carnivorous Plant Society
(www.carnivorousplants.org)
Find out about carnivorous plants and
efforts to save them worldwide.

Your First Bog Garden
(www.suite101.com/article.cfm/
enabling_garden/2778)
Learn how to plant a bog garden
with carnivorous plants.

Index